NATIONAL GEOGRAPHIC

THE HUMAN BODY

Bones and Muscles

REBECCA L. JOHNSON

PICTURE CREDITS
Cover (bkgd) International Stock/ImageState. Page 1 (bkgd) Owen
Franklin/Corbis; page 2 (bkgd) Tim Pannell/Corbis; page 4 (bottom) Tony
Freeman/PhotoEdit, Inc.; page 4 (top) Tom Stewart/Corbis; page 5 David
Young-Wolf/PhotoEdit, Inc.; page 6 (bottom left) Dave Roberts/Science Photo
Library/Photo Researchers, Inc.; page 6 (top) Photograph by Patrick Nduru
Gathogo, University of Utah; page 6 (bottom right) Kenneth Garrett/Kenya
National Museum; page 7 Stockbyte; page 8 (bottom left) Science Photo
Library/Photo Researchers, Inc.; pages 8, 10, 12-13, 19, 26 art by Stephen
Durke; page 9 Bill Bachman/Photo Researchers, Inc.; page 10 (bkgd), 11
Royalty-Free/Corbis; pages 12-13 (bkgd) Photodisc Green/Getty Images;
page 14 (bottom) Paul Barton/Corbis; page 14 (top left) Stephen Dalton/Photo
Researchers, Inc.; page 14 (top right) John Karapelou, CMI/Phototake; pages 15,
27, 28, 29 Matt Meadows/Matt Meadows Photography; page 16 (left) Felicia
Martinez/Photo Edit, Inc.; page 16 (bottom right) Custom Medical Stock ; page
16 (middle right) E. R. Degginger/Bruce Coleman, Inc.; page 16 (top right) Phil
Degginger/Bruce Coleman, Inc.; page 17 Liane Cary/AGE Fotostock; page 18
(bottom) Globus, Holway & Lobel/Corbis; page 18 (top left) Digital Vision; page
19 (bottom right) David Madison/Bruce Coleman, Inc.; page 20 (top left) James
Stevenson/Science Photo Library/Photo Researchers, Inc.; page 20 (right) James
King-Holmes/Science Photo Library/Photo Researchers, Inc.; page 20 (bottom
left) Lon C. Diehl/PhotoEdit, Inc.; page 21 Michael Kelley Photography; page 22
(top left), 23 (bottom right) AP/Wide World; page 23 (top) AFP/Corbis; page 23
(bottom left) Image Courtesy of Otto Bock; page 24 (top) Photograph by Kaku
Kurita; page 25 (top) Mark E. Gibson/Corbis; page 25 (bottom) Image Source.

Neither the publisher nor the author shall be liable for any damage that may be
caused or sustained or result from conducting any of the activities in this book
without specifically following instructions, undertaking the activities without
proper supervision, or failing to comply with the cautions contained in the book.

Produced through the worldwide resources of the National Geographic Society,
John M. Fahey, Jr. President and Chief Executive Officer; Gilbert M. Grosvenor,
Chairman of the Board; Nina D. Hoffman, Executive Vice President and
President, Books and Education Publishing Group.

PREPARED BY NATIONAL GEOGRAPHIC SCHOOL PUBLISHING
Ericka Markman, Senior Vice President and President, Children's Books and
Education Publishing Group; Steve Mico, Vice President, Editorial Director;
Rosemary Baker, Executive Editor; Barbara Seeber, Editorial Manager; Jim
Hiscott, Design Manager; Kristin Hanneman, Illustrations Manager; Matt
Wascavage, Manager of Publishing Services; Sean Philpotts, Production
Coordinator.

MANUFACTURING AND QUALITY MANAGEMENT
Chief Financial Officer, Christopher A. Liedel; Director, Phillip L. Schlosser;
Manager, Clifton M. Brown.

PROGRAM DEVELOPER
Kate Boehm Jerome

ART DIRECTION
Daniel Banks, Project Design Company

CONSULTANT/REVIEWER
Dr. Kathleen Marrs, Assistant Professor of Biology, Indiana University Purdue
University Indianapolis

BOOK DEVELOPMENT
The Mazer Corporation

Published by the National Geographic Society
Washington, D.C. 20036-4688

Product No. 4J41779

ISBN: 978-0-7922-4585-8
ISBN: 0-7922-4585-7

Printed in U.S.A.

19 18 17 16 15 14 13
10 9 8 7 6 5 4

Contents

Strength and Structure

. . . eighteen, nineteen, . . . and . . . you did it!
Twenty push-ups. Last week you could do only ten.
Your muscles are getting stronger. Just feel that
bulge on top of your arm!

That bulge has a name: your *biceps*. It's a big muscle that is attached to bones in your arm. You can bend your arm only because your biceps muscle is connected to the bones in your lower arm. Without your biceps, your arm would just hang limply at your side.

Without bones, of course, your entire body would be limp—a sort of shapeless, rubbery blob. Like girders in a building, bones are the framework of your body. They give it structure and form. But bones can't move without the help of muscles.

This is a book about muscles and bones. They are pretty important— without them you couldn't pet your cat, kick a soccer ball, swim laps, or even take a breath. Let's take a closer look at these remarkable body parts.

Chapter 1

A Fantastic Framework

Anthropologist Meave Leakey finds skull

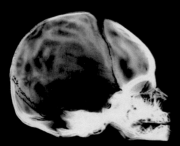

X-ray of baby's skull

Researcher assembling fossil skull of *Kenyanthropus*

The researchers carefully brushed away the sand. Bit by bit the bones came into view. It was a fossil skull! But how old was it?

In 1999 a team of scientists working in Kenya, East Africa, discovered an ancient skull unlike anything seen before. When the bones were dated, they turned out to be roughly 3.5 million years old. The scientists believe that the bones belong to a previously unknown ancestor of humans. They named their find *Kenyanthropus platyops,* which means "flat-faced person of Kenya."

The fossil bones of *Kenyanthropus* are solid and hard, like rock. They look dry and dead. But at one time those bones were very much alive, just like the bones in your body. Bones are complex organs that are growing and changing all the time.

Believe it or not, even the *number* of bones in your body changes. You were born with about 270 bones. As you grew, some of those bones joined together, including those that make up your skull. Now you've got a total of about 206 bones, give or take a few!

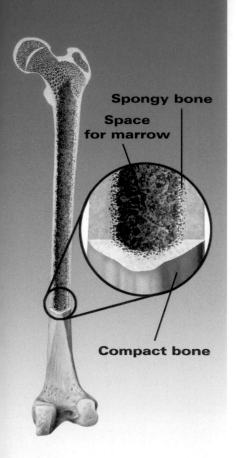

Spongy bone

Space
for marrow

Compact bone

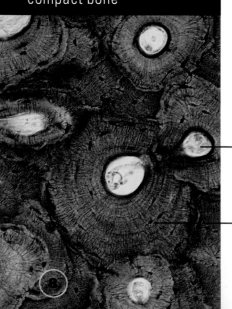

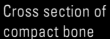

Space for
blood vessel

Bone cell

Inside a Bone

From the outside, bones look smooth and solid. But there's more to bones than meets the eye. If you could cut into a living bone, you'd discover that it's made up of several different layers.

The outer layer is called **compact bone**. Under a microscope, compact bone looks like a group of tube-shaped units that are tightly packed together. Bone cells live in these units, surrounded by a hard framework. The framework contains **minerals,** primarily calcium and phosphorus.

Beneath the layer of compact bone lies **spongy bone**. While compact bone is solid, spongy bone is full of spaces, like the holes in a sponge. Because of all the holes, spongy bone is fairly lightweight. But it's still mineral-rich and hard.

In some of your bones, spongy bone surrounds an open space. This space is filled with bone **marrow**. Marrow looks a bit like fatty red jelly. It's not very pretty, but it's essential to your survival. Why? Bone marrow produces red blood cells—at the incredible rate of about two million per second!

Breaking Down and Building Up

Although you can't see or feel it happening, your bones are constantly changing. They are being remodeled, like an old house that is being updated. Let's see how this works.

Your bones have two basic kinds of cells. One kind of bone cell acts as a sort of demolition team. These bone destroyers break down the mineral-rich framework of compact and spongy bone. They help release calcium and phosphorus in the process.

The second kind of bone cell is responsible for making new bone. These bone builders use minerals to construct new compact and spongy bone. At any given moment, the first type of cell is breaking down bone while the second type is building it up again. In a healthy person, these breaking-down and building-up processes are in balance.

Why does your body go to all this trouble? Remodeling keeps bones healthier and stronger than they would be if they always stayed the same. And when bone is broken down, calcium and phosphorus are released. Some of these minerals enter your blood and are carried to nerves, muscles, and other body parts that need those minerals to function. Bone remodeling keeps these important minerals on the move.

Stay Tuned!

Fix It with Foam

What do F-18 fighter jets and broken bones have in common? Both may benefit from a new kind of synthetic foam. The rigid, lightweight foam was originally designed to surround and protect jet airplane antennas. But it's as strong and sturdy as human bone. Doctors hope that small pieces of this new foam can be implanted in badly broken bones. The foam implants would create a framework on which bone-building cells could settle and grow. The result? Bones that mend more quickly!

Skeleton Keys

Bones come in all sorts of shapes and sizes. Some are long and narrow with rounded ends, like the bone in your upper arm. Some are flat, thin, and broad, like your shoulder blades. Some are small and stubby, like your wrist bones. And some, like the bones that are stacked to form your backbone, have irregular shapes that defy description. The biggest bone in the human body is the femur, or thigh bone. The smallest bone is in an unexpected place—inside your ear!

Together, all the bones in your body form your **skeleton,** or skeletal system. The skeleton is like a building's framework of girders, rafters, and beams. It holds up your body and gives it shape.

But that's not all. Your skeleton also protects your internal organs. Your ribs, for instance, form a "cage" in your chest. Nestled safely inside this bony structure are some of your most vital organs, including your heart, lungs, and liver. The bones in your skeleton also are the places where many of your muscles attach. (More on muscles in a moment). Check out the key functions of your skeleton in the table at left.

Where Bones Meet

The place in a skeleton where two or more bones come together is called a **joint**. Some joints are fixed—they don't move. Moving joints, on the other hand, are those that allow you to twist, bend, and move parts of your body in hundreds of different ways. Bones in moving joints are held together by **ligaments**. These tough strands of tissue are like very strong rubber bands.

But although ligaments are strong, they have their limits. If enough stress is put on a ligament, it can tear. Many sports injuries involve torn ligaments, often in the knee. Athletes place tremendous stresses on their knees as they run, jump, pivot, and kick. Knees are designed to bend backward, not forward or from side to side!

Bones and the ligaments that hold them together are like parts of a finely tuned machine. If you treat them with care, they will last a long time.

Athlete with trainer

I.Q. Interesting Question

Q. Why do knuckles and some other joints occasionally "crack"?

A. Some of your joints, like your knuckles, are surrounded by a little bag of tissue that's full of thick, clear fluid. The fluid helps lubricate the joints so that they will work smoothly. The fluid also contains dissolved gases. When you crack a knuckle, you're pushing the joint either back into or out of its normal position. That changes the pressure on the fluid. The pressure change causes tiny bubbles of dissolved gas to form in the fluid— similar to what happens when you open a can of soda. The bubbles of gas burst, making a popping sound.

How Do Broken Bones Heal?

Bones are strong. But if enough pressure is put on it, even the strongest bone can break. Any crack or break in a bone is called a *fracture*.

The good news is that bones can repair themselves. The two kinds of bone cells you met before—bone destroyers and bone builders—play a major role in this process. Let's explore how a broken bone heals.

Bone-building cells at work

Spongy bone

Hematoma

Compact bone

Muscle

2 **Bone building begins.** Next, bone cells move into the fracture zone. Bone-building bone cells go to work joining the broken ends of the bone together. The hematoma slowly hardens around the break, strengthening the injured area.

1 **Hematoma forms.** When a bone breaks, many blood vessels are damaged. Blood flows into the area of the break and forms a **hematoma**, which is a swollen area that closes off the injured blood vessels and stops the bleeding.

New spongy bone

New compact bone

❸ Spongy bone forms. Gradually, the bone-building bone cells build a bridge of spongy bone between the two broken ends, splicing them together. At the same time, bone-destroying bone cells eat away the hardened hematoma.

❹ Compact bone forms. Over the next few months, the two kinds of bone cells work together to remodel the fracture zone. The spongy bone is broken down and replaced by compact bone. Within about a year, the bone will be almost as strong as it was before the break. The only sign that the bone was broken is a slight thickening at the old fracture site.

Chapter 2   Marvelous Muscles

Human knee joint

The year was 1786. In his laboratory, Luigi Galvani was studying a dissected frog. An assistant accidentally touched the frog's leg with a metal scalpel. There was a spark. The dead frog's leg muscles twitched violently. Galvani had just discovered that electricity can cause a muscle to contract.

Muscles make bones and other body parts move. They accomplish this amazing feat by **contracting,** or getting shorter. Contracting muscles make it possible for you to laugh, run, dance, do cartwheels, catch a ball, and move in countless other ways. They also pump blood around your body and help you digest your food. Muscles are definitely multitalented!

The secret to muscle power lies in the structure of the muscle. Muscles are made up of bundles of tiny, stretchy fibers. The fibers are intertwined the way you might interlace your fingers. When a muscle gets a message to contract, the fibers slide closer together. The muscle gets shorter and pulls on whatever it's attached to. Many contractions taking place at the same time add up to a powerful force that can really make things move.

Your body is home to hundreds of muscles. They make up nearly half of your body weight. You can control some of these muscles. Others do their jobs without your thinking about them at all.

Muscle fibers intertwine just as your fingers do when you clasp your hands.

Kinds of Muscles

You have three kinds of muscles in your body: smooth, cardiac, and skeletal muscles. Under a microscope, they look slightly different. But every muscle has the power to contract and make things move.

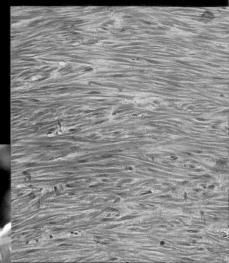

Cardiac muscle

Skeletal muscle

Muscles work to move food and liquid down your esophagus every time you swallow.

Smooth Moves

Smooth muscles work behind the scenes in your body. They are found in the walls of most internal organs. They line blood vessels and lie hidden in your skin.

What do smooth muscles do? A lot of them help move substances through your body. For example, smooth muscles in blood vessels work to keep blood flowing to every part of your body. Smooth muscles in your stomach contract to mix food with digestive juices. When your stomach is empty, it's those same contracting muscles that make your stomach "growl."

When you get chilled—or scared—tiny smooth muscles in your skin contract, raising the hair on your skin and giving you goose bumps!

The Beat Goes On

Cardiac muscle is found only in the thick walls of your heart. With every beat, cardiac muscles contract to pump blood through the heart and out into your body. Cardiac muscle never rests. The average person's heart beats about 72 times per minute. That's 4,320 times an hour and 103,680 times a day! Your heart began beating before you were born and won't stop until the last moment of your life.

Both smooth muscle and cardiac muscle are called **involuntary** muscle. You can't control when or how hard or how fast they contract. Parts of your brain and body tell these muscles what to do. You never have to think about it.

Thinking Like a Scientist:

Observing

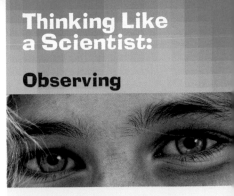

The dark spot in the center of your eye is the pupil. It's an opening that allows light to enter. Tiny smooth muscles change the pupil's size. To observe these involuntary muscles at work, try this:

- Stand in front of a mirror. The room should be dimly lit.
- Observe the size of both of your pupils.
- Now, using a small flashlight (not a laser pointer), slowly move a beam of light across one side of your face. Make sure that it shines directly into the pupil of one eye. Immediately turn off the light.
- Recheck the size of your pupils.

What happened to your pupils when you shined the light? After the light went out, did your pupils change size again? Why do you think this happened?

The Bone Movers

Skeletal muscles are the muscles that move your bones. When you brush your teeth or throw a baseball, skeletal muscles make the movement possible. Skeletal muscles are **voluntary**—these are muscles you *can* control.

The human body contains more than 600 skeletal muscles. Some, like those in your eyelids, are attached to skin. Most skeletal muscles, however, attach to bones by strong cords of tissue called **tendons**.

Skeletal muscles come in different shapes and sizes depending on the job they do. Your largest and strongest muscles are in your back. Their main job is to help you stand upright. For their size, however, the strongest muscles in your body are your jaw muscles. When they contract, they allow you to bite down with surprising force!

Working in Pairs

In order to move bones back and forth at a joint, some skeletal muscles work in pairs. When one member of the pair contracts, the bone moves in one direction. When the other member of the muscle pair contracts, the bone moves in the opposite direction.

Want to give this a try? Stand up and bend your leg at the knee as if you are winding up to kick a soccer ball. Do you feel the muscles in the back of your leg contract? As the muscles contract, they pull your lower leg bones up and back. Now pretend to kick the ball. The muscles in the back of your thigh relax as the ones in front of your thigh suddenly contract. Your lower leg comes down—with enough power to send the ball soaring!

Skeletal muscles work with your bones to give your body speed and strength. Caring for your muscles is just as important as caring for your bones. One of the best ways to do that is to use your muscles every day. Take a walk, ride your bike, carry the groceries, swim laps, and yes, do push-ups! The more you use your muscles, the stronger they will be. Together with strong bones, strong muscles will carry you through life with ease.

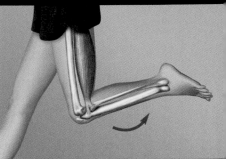

Muscles in back of thigh contract and pull leg up

Muscles in front of thigh contract and straighten lower leg

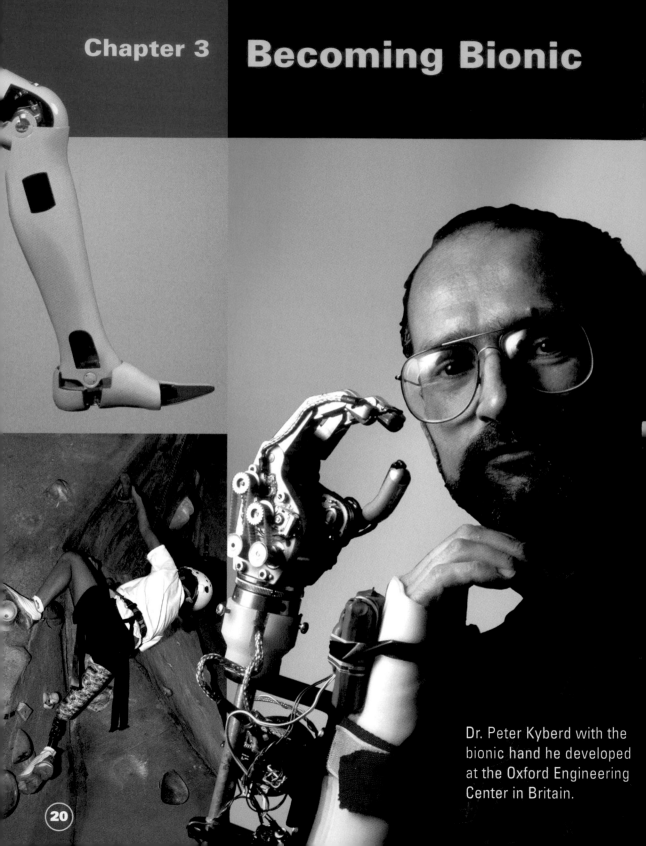

Chapter 3

Becoming Bionic

Dr. Peter Kyberd with the bionic hand he developed at the Oxford Engineering Center in Britain.

Carry 400 pounds with ease. Leap tall fences in a single bound. Run for miles without breaking a sweat. Sound impossible? Not if you're wearing an Exoskeleton!

An Exoskeleton is a robot-like suit that can be strapped onto a person's body. The suit senses the muscle contractions of the person wearing it. Then it adds mechanical power to enhance natural movements. There's enough power to turn the average person into a superhuman!

Exoskeletons are still in the experimental stage. But already on the market is an amazing collection of bionic devices, from artificial limbs and joints to hearts. A **bionic** device is an electronic or mechanical piece of equipment that replaces a real body part.

Everyone hopes that his or her muscles and bones will last a lifetime. But as people age, these structures sometimes deteriorate. Diseases and injuries can make them stop functioning, or they can be lost altogether. Bionic devices offer people who are missing an arm, a leg, or some other body part the chance to live a more normal life. Breakthroughs in technology are making bionics better all the time.

Soldier wearing an experimental Exoskeleton

Sir Ludwig Guttmann: Founder of the Paralympics

In 1948 Dr. Ludwig Guttmann, a doctor at Stoke Mandeville Hospital in England, organized a sports competition for World War II veterans with spinal cord injuries. In the years that followed, disabled competitors from Europe joined in. In 1976 the idea of bringing together athletes with disabilities from around the world for an international sports competition led to the official creation of the Paralympic Games. As a result of his efforts, Dr. Guttmann has been called the Father of Sports for the Disabled.

Computer Parts

If you lost your leg in an accident a hundred years ago, your only hope for a replacement would have been a stiff wooden leg. Today's artificial legs are made of super-strong, lightweight metals such as aluminum and titanium. These limbs have complex joints. Many are covered in plastics that look like skin. Now the challenge is to make artificial limbs that move as smoothly as real limbs.

The C-leg is a big step forward. The C stands for computer. This bionic leg contains a computer chip and sensors that make adjustments to the leg—about 50 times per second—so that it moves naturally, just as a real leg does. The goal of the C-leg's inventors is to make the bionic limb feel like a natural part of a person's body.

Just Think About It

Other scientists are working on bionic limbs that can be controlled by a person's brain waves. In other words, you can make the limb move in a certain way just by thinking about it. This relatively new area of research is called **neuroprosthetics**. Operating something outside your body with brain waves sounds a little bit like science fiction. But new advances in computer technology are turning thought-controlled prosthetics into scientific fact.

Shea Cowart won the Paralympics women's 100-meter race in 2000.

A C-leg

Mihoko Otake
in her Tokyo lab

Gel Power!

Scientists are also experimenting with new ways to make artificial limbs move. Japanese researcher Mihoko Otake has created a synthetic "starfish" out of a special kind of gel. The gel changes shape in response to an electric field. You can demonstrate an electric field by rubbing the surface of a blown-up balloon on your shirt and then holding the balloon close to your head. Your hair will bend out toward the balloon. It's being pulled by an electric field.

Using tiny field-generating electrodes, Dr. Otake can make her rubbery creature move in different ways. It can even do a somersault!

The Dancing Starfish

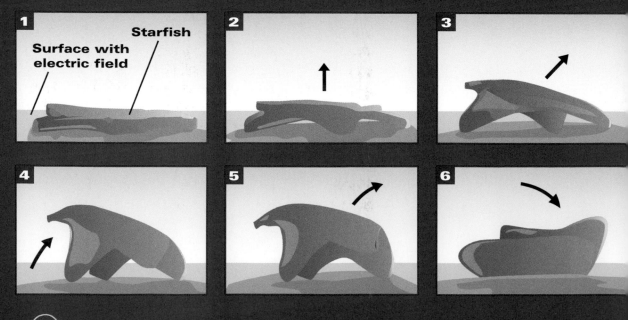

1
Surface with
electric field

Starfish

2

3

4

5

6

How useful is a somersaulting synthetic starfish? It's actually an important first step on the road toward creating new types of artificial muscles. Such muscles may one day power artificial limbs, allowing them to move smoothly and naturally—just like the real thing.

Scientific advances like these offer hope of a more normal life to thousands of people who need artificial limbs and other body parts. And who knows? By the time you get old, "being bionic" may be as common as wearing glasses or contacts is today. In the meantime, take good care of your body. There's nothing out there yet that can truly replace your marvelous muscles and remarkable bones!

Observing

You've probably seen your face in a mirror thousands of times. But have you ever really *observed* that familiar face as a scientist would? Observing is more than just looking. It means looking very carefully, noticing every detail.

Practice the Skill

Beneath the skin of your face is an amazing set of muscles. You can't actually see them, but you can observe what they do when they contract. Study the illustration below. It shows the major

Muscles of the Head and Neck

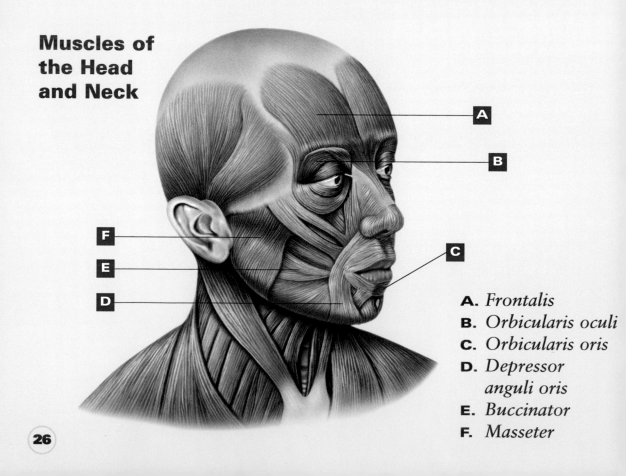

A. Frontalis
B. Orbicularis oculi
C. Orbicularis oris
D. Depressor anguli oris
E. Buccinator
F. Masseter

muscles of the head and neck. (You've got a set just like these!) Then follow the steps to help you observe what different facial muscles can do.

1. Pucker up as though you're going to kiss someone. What happens to the shape of your mouth? Which muscle do you think is contracting so that you can do this?

2. Blow air out of your mouth as if you are blowing out a candle. Observe the shape of your cheeks. The muscle labeled E helps them puff out like that.

3. Smile. Which muscle do you think is helping turn up the corners of your mouth?

4. Close your mouth. Put your hand on the side of your face and grit your teeth (clench your jaw). Which muscle can you feel contracting?

5. Close one eye. You can thank the muscle labeled B for that. Find it on the illustration.

6. Raise your eyebrows as high as you can so that your forehead is wrinkled horizontally. Which muscle is helping you make this expression?

Check It Out!

Without moving your head, look from side to side. Now look up and down. Finally, move your eyes around in a complete circle, like the minute hand of a clock. Feel the muscles moving your eyes? Each eye has three pairs of muscles that control eye movement. They are some of the most quickly contracting and most precisely controlled skeletal muscles in your body!

"Calcium builds strong bones." How often have you heard that? But is calcium really that important? Try this activity to see what happens to bones when calcium disappears.

Explore

1 Test the flexibility of the chicken bone by gently trying to bend it with your fingers. Do not press so hard that you break the bone.

2 Place the bone in the jar.

3 Fill the jar with enough vinegar to cover the bone completely.

Materials
- 1 clean, dry chicken leg bone
- Quart glass jar, with lid
- White vinegar
- Paper towels
- Paper, pencil

4 Screw the lid on the jar.

CAUTION: WIPE UP ANY SPILLS WITH PAPER TOWELS, AND WASH YOUR HANDS.

5 The next day, take the bone out of the jar and test its flexibility again with your fingers. Record your observations. Replace the bone in the vinegar, put the lid on the jar, and wash your hands.

6 Repeat step 5 every day for a week.

Think

Vinegar is an acid. It reacts chemically with bone, removing calcium from it.

After seven days, how much more flexible is the bone than it was when you began the activity?

What conclusions can you draw about how calcium affects a bone's strength?

Science Notebook

Bone Facts

- Your skeleton is actually made of two skeletons. One is composed of the bones of your head, spine, and rib cage. The other comprises the bones of your arms, hands, pelvis, legs, and feet.

- Exercise every day. Exercising stimulates bone-building bone cells to work harder.

- Include milk and other dairy products in your diet every day. The calcium in these foods really does strengthen your bones.

Websites to Visit

Take a quiz and watch an animation about muscles and how they work. *http://www.brainpop.com/health/muscular/muscular/index.weml?&tried_cookie=true*

View individual bones of the human skeleton— some from every angle. *www.eskeletons.org*

Meet Yorick, the bionic skeleton. *www.fda.gov/oc/opacom/kids/html/yorick_no.1.htm* Click on Yorick's various bionic parts to learn more about how they work.

Books to Read

Treays, Rebecca. *Understanding Your Muscles & Bones* (Science for Beginners Series). E D C Publications, 1997.

Levert, Suzanne. *Bones and Muscles* (Kaleidoscope). Benchmark Books, 2001.

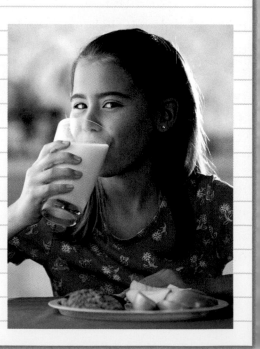

Glossary

bionic (*bye-AH-nick*) – having both biological and electronic parts

cardiac muscle (*CAR-dee-ack MUH-suhl*) – heart muscle

compact bone – hard material that forms the outside layer of bones

contract(ing) – drawing together, making smaller

fracture (*FRACK-chur*) – to break or crack

hematoma (*hee-mah-TOE-mah*) – clotted blood that forms in tissue

involuntary (*in-VAHL-uhn-tare-ee*) – not controlled, not done on purpose

joint – place where two bones join

ligament (*LIG-uh-muhnt*) – tissue that connects two bones

marrow – soft tissue inside large bones

mineral – chemical element, such as calcium or phosphorus, that the body needs for life processes

neuroprosthetics (*nyoor-oh-prahs-THET-icks*) – devices implanted into the brain or nervous system to repair problems or expand capabilities

skeletal muscle – muscles responsible for voluntary movement

skeleton – the body's framework of bones

smooth muscle – muscles found in internal organs, not under voluntary control

spongy bone – less dense material that makes up the inside of bones

tendon (*TEN-duhn*) – tissue that connects muscle to bone or other body tissue

voluntary – under control, done on purpose

Index